The Chicken or the Egg?

By Allan Fowler

Consultants:
Robert L. Hillerich, Ph.D., Bowling Green
State University, Bowling Green, Ohio

Mary Nalbandian, Director of Science,
Chicago Public Schools, Chicago, Illinois

Fay Robinson, Child Development Specialist

CHILDRENS PRESS®
CHICAGO

Design by Beth Herman Design Associates

Library of Congress Cataloging-in-Publication Data

Fowler, Allan
    The chicken or the egg? / by Allan Fowler.
        p. cm. –(Rookie read-about science)
    Summary: A brief look at the physical characteristics, breeds, and
    habits of chickens and at how modern poultry farms produce eggs
    and chickens.
        ISBN 0-516-06008-2
        1. Chickens–Juvenile literature. 2. Eggs–Juvenile literature.
    [1. Chickens. 2. Eggs] I. Title. II. Series: Fowler, Allan.
    Rookie read-about science.
SF487.5.F69 1993
636.5–dc20   92-35054
                                                                 CIP
                                                                  AC

A long time ago, certain
brightly colored birds lived
in the jungles in faraway Asia.

Then people started keeping them around their homes – because the birds were good to eat. And so were the eggs they laid.

Little by little, those birds changed – until over the years they became the chickens we know today.

Birds that are raised for food – such as chickens, turkeys, ducks, and geese – are known as poultry.

The people who keep
chickens are poultry farmers.

A single poultry farm
may have thousands and
thousands of chickens.

Plymouth Rocks and Rhode Island Reds are just two breeds of chickens.

There are many other breeds.

A male chicken is called a rooster. A female chicken is called a hen.

All chickens have combs on top of their heads and wattles under their beaks. On a rooster, the comb and wattle are larger.

Roosters crow –
Cock-a-doodle-doo!
Hens cluck.

And baby chickens peep.

Farmers make sure their chickens get just the right corn and grains to grow big and healthy.

Some breeds lay eggs with brown shells. Some lay eggs with white shells.

Brown eggs and white eggs taste the same.

A laying hen lays about five eggs a week.

The eggs you eat are unfertilized eggs.
That means there are no baby chicks growing inside the eggs.

21

If an egg is fertilized,
the hen sits on it to keep
it warm until it hatches.

But on modern poultry
farms, fertilized eggs are
put in incubators right
after they are laid.

Think about how hot it is
on a very hot summer day.
It is always like that in an
incubator.

After three weeks, the egg
hatches.

25

The baby chick pecks its way out of the shell.

It is wet and tired. But,
after a nap, it is ready
to feed itself and to start
growing up.

If anyone asks you, "Which came first, the chicken or the egg?" – here's one answer you can give: "The egg!

Because we eat eggs for breakfast – and chicken for dinner."